RUNNING FOR THE SOUL 2

MORE STORIES OF TRIUMPH

ALL FROM RUNNERS LIKE YOU

ROAD RUNNER SPORTS®

Acknowledgements

Edited by Claudia Piepenburg

Graphic Design by Beata Csanadi, Grafikus

Cover Design by Joan Maloney, Studio Three One Eight

Printing by Diego & Son

Quotations from *The Book of Positive Quotations*, compiled and arranged by Jon Cook (Fairview Press, Minneapolis, MN, 1993)

Additional quotations from *Random Acts of Kindness*, the editors of Conari Press (Foreward by Daphne Rose Kingma, Conari Press, Berkeley, CA, 1993)

Introduction

Do you remember why you started running?

Maybe you wanted to lose weight, or you made a bet with someone that you could run a 10K. Maybe you had been sick and you started running to celebrate your recovery. Or maybe a loved one passed away and you trained for and ran a marathon to honor them.

Maybe you accompanied your spouse or a friend on a run one day and discovered how good it felt to breathe, really breathe, deeply and powerfully; to feel the sun warming your face and the wind stroking your hair. Perhaps you fell in love with the way you felt when you threw in a little surge at the end of the run; a surge that led to a long, loving relationship with a new you . . . a strong and energetic athlete.

Read well the stories that follow; you may find yourself in one of them. Or you may discover new reasons to love running even more than ever before. The stories tell the tale . . . you'll learn that running links us all in marvelous and, sometimes, miraculous ways.

See you on the road!

Mike G.

Mike Gotfredson
Chief Runner

P.S. *Running for the Soul 3* will be all about women and running. Send your motivational, inspirational and unique running stories to cpiepe@roadrunnersports.com.

SECTION I

REFLECTION

Never put off until tomorrow
what you can do today,
because if you enjoy it today,
you can do it again, tomorrow.

— Anonymous

Roadside Reflections

5:50 AM comes early as usual, announcing its arrival with the voice of National Public Radio losing ground only to the loud purring of Gryphon, the cat, nestled evenly just below my chin. Rolling out of bed I try not to think of the morning's chill and successfully make it downstairs into the kitchen. As I get dressed Gryphon lovingly brushes up against my legs, reminding me it's never too early to be fed. After a little food and a quick pet, I quietly sneak out the door so as to not wake the anxieties of the day.

No one is in sight. The day's light has not yet taken control of the world. In a sea of parked cars, I'm surrounded by towering, non-descript buildings. My only companion is the silence that surrounds me. My sluggish brain hasn't yet been fully charged. Checking my timer I begin to slowly stride through the intersection that will be crowded with cars in a few hours. It's so quiet.

The external world slowly fades out of my perception and the sound of my feet begin to syncopate the beats of my heart and the in-and-out rhythm of my lungs. The first ten minutes is marked with signs of fatigue, signaling that the jog will soon become a run. The Quiet Waters Reservoir is in my sight. A silhouette of homes lines up to my left, still and motionless, asleep. As I blend into the tapestry of the woods around me, I move like a metronome down the curving trail, getting lost in the hum of my body.

My mind starts to come alive, spewing mental snapshots of things I need to do and reviewing the days before. Did I ask the right question in the seminar? Did I read Spinoza closely enough? Will Newton become my best friend in senior year? Watch out, there's a tree limb! How can I be a better man? Where will today take me and where will I be in ten years? So many squirrels! Am I

making a difference? What does it all mean? Am
I a man of vice or virtue?

All these thoughts are siphoning into my brain
as I slow down to take in the morning's dancing
lights over the South River. As dawn sweeps in,
the wood's tenants stop their cheerful chores and
scurry to their burrows for a day of slumber. I'm
making it around my loop and now the homes are
wide-awake with activity. The solitude I experi-
enced in the morning's blanket of shade has been
lifted and lost in the roar of wheels and movement.

The morning is gone and the day has taken
over. As I approach the end of my run, the sea of
cars has dwindled away; those few left are eagerly
waiting for their owners to appear with ice scraper
in hand. My home, too, is lit up. I can faintly hear
Alexa starting her day, getting dressed upstairs.
Gryphon is contently draping the seat of the kitchen
chair, letting me know she's glad I'm back, and I
had better start the coffee. In the corner of my
eye I see my schoolbooks glaring at me and am
reminded that I can run, but I can't always hide
— at least until tomorrow.

Written by Michael Behmer
New York, New York

A Universe Away

I, like many others, run to clear my mind. To be transported far from the worries of the day, and to maintain my healthy lifestyle through the best possible exercise.

There's a Wisconsin countryside run that lifts my spirits like no other. It's six miles, winding up and down and around rolling fields of corn, soy, and alfalfa. The cows I see run with me, along the edge of their fence line, as if they wish for the freedom I have. There are several spots along the route where you can see miles and miles of patchwork farmland, dotted with silos and farmhouses.

One typical hot and humid summer day, with late thunderstorms predicted, I came home from work quite harried from a particularly stressful afternoon. My family said they would hold supper while I ran off my day. (They like me better after a run than after work, as they have a vested interest in my sanity.) So, I stretched, hydrated and off I went.

> **The cows I see run with me, along the edge of their fence line, as if they wish for the freedom I have.**

About half way into my run I had the option to cut two miles from the total distance by taking a shortcut home. I was sweating heavily, but feeling great, and thunder was rumbling in the distance, echoing off the rolling landscape. I knew the smart thing to do was to cut the run short — but sometimes I don't make smart decisions. The scene was too beautiful to end just because of a few peals of thunder. Besides, the anvil-shaped clouds responsible for that breathtaking symphony seemed to be running parallel to my course.

No surprise, at mile four, the heavens opened. Not a light sprinkle, but a deluge. I picked up the

pace in order to get home quickly, but then . . .
I slowed down. I was soaked clear through to the
bones. I couldn't possibly get any wetter. I realized that the rain was one of those warm summer
washes that don't feel chilly, but instead warm you
like a cleansing shower. I smiled. The remarkable
run had carried me away from my aching thighs
and sore knee, away from angry customers and
a stressful commute. I think I flew home.

The rain stopped when I was about one hundred feet from home. The dry pavement told me
that the storm had just missed my house. I had
visions of my family being worried (or amused)
that I had been caught in the storm. I imagined
them peering through the front window, waiting
for my return.

But they weren't aware of the storm. Their
afternoon routine seemed a universe away from
my run in the rain. It felt almost as if nothing had
happened.

"Daddy, why are you all wet?"

"Am I?"

*My name is Dave Schmitz. I'm thirty-six years old. I live in south-
east Wisconsin (where I was born and raised) with my wife, Beth,
four children and a dog named Einstein. I'm training for my
second marathon.*

You cannot step twice

into the same river,

for other waters are

continually flowing on.

— Heraclitus

Another Reason

5:30 AM — I head out the door into the frigid air and the symphony begins.

The lonely, empty streets simulate a concert hall. The music commences with the faint, soft "pit pat" of the snowflakes as they join the fresh snow already covering the lawns. Mixing together with the "pit pat" is the "clop clop" of my shoes as they strike the wet pavement, mingled with the "swish swish" of my jacket as my arms move against my sides.

Every few minutes there's a crescendo — "splash," as my foot encounters a puddle that I poorly navigated. Underneath it all I can hear my breathing "whoo . . . whoo." Rhythmic, balanced and steady.

For one hour, the glorious music continues . . .

"pit pat"

"clop clop"

"swish swish"

splash

"whoo . . . whoo"

Near the end of my run, the climactic finale of the symphony bellows with the thunderous rattling of the cars when they pass me and the hissing of their tires on the soaked road. Rush hour traffic has invaded the morning.

As I turn into my driveway, I wonder what I would name this magnificent piece of music if I were a composer. And it comes to me. I would call it: "Another Day, Another Reason to Run."

Written by Kristen Flabiano
Dallas, Texas

Remember the
Embarcadero Freeway?

I'll never forget the Embarcadero Freeway in San Francisco. It was about forty or fifty feet high and had been recently sentenced to demolition because of earthquake damage.

It was a brisk early morning with, surprisingly for San Francisco, no fog. I jogged up the on-ramp and ran up through the Financial District, all the while watching the sunrise from beyond the Sierra Mountains and the golden rays glowing and growing on the skyscrapers. A whole four-lane highway to myself, watching the traffic below wake up to a new morning. Yahoo! What an energizing morning!

My name is Chris Brong. I'm a Federal Game Warden for the District of Columbia, Maryland and Delaware area. I've run regularly for both on-the-job energy and overall fitness since 1978.

Turkey Trot

One morning I was running with a couple of my running club buddies. We were running a nine-mile run on a bicycle path through a wooded park. Suddenly, in front of us we noticed a flock of about five or six wild turkeys. Usually when we saw wildlife on the trail, they would scurry off into the underbrush very quickly. However, this time the turkeys started to run in front of us. Their little legs were pumping like crazy! They would put a little distance between themselves and us, then they would start to walk. As soon as we got close again, they would start running. This continued for some time. Those turkeys ran with us for about a mile, before finally taking off into the woods.

Ever since that day, we've referred to that experience as our "turkey trot" because it happened right around Thanksgiving.

My name is Richard Clark. I'm a forty-three year old with two children (Crystal, age thirteen, and Daniel, age six) living in New Port Richey, Florida. I'm president of the Starkey Runners Club. It's a small running club that meets every week to run in a wooded park (the same park where the turkey trot took place).

It's not that

"today is the first day

of the rest of my life,"

but that now is

all there is of my life.

— Hugh Prather

SECTION II

INSPIRATION

Seek those who find your

road agreeable, your personality

and mind stimulating, your

philosophy acceptable, and

your experiences helpful.

Let those who do not,

seek their own kind.

— Jean-Henri Fabre

Michael . . . Thanks

My inspiration is my husband, Michael. He has been running two years to my twenty. He started out slowly on a basement treadmill, not wanting to venture outside where he might be seen. He advanced to 5Ks and 10Ks rather quickly, but balked at the thought of running longer distances. Then he began helping me train for the 2000 Dublin Marathon and, in the process, decided to run half of it with me.

He couldn't have picked a more difficult race. It was cold and raining with intense headwinds. But he made it through his half in good shape. In May of this year he ran his first official half marathon, the Indy 5000 Mini, finishing in a respectable 2:17. I was sure he was done for the season, as he isn't a hot weather kind of guy, but he suggested we run a local marathon relay just one month after the Mini. I was delighted.

The weather for the race was predicted to be cool in the morning, so I let him run the first half. I cheered him on as he crossed the start line, then I boarded the bus that would take the second-half runners to the 13.1-mile marker. I figured I had plenty of time, at least two hours and seventeen minutes before I would switch places with Michael, but I made sure I was ready long beforehand. It's a good thing I did. Two hours and four minutes into the race I was checking my shoes, doing some stretches, and watching other runners come and go. I looked

> I figured I had plenty of time, at least two hours and seventeen minutes before I would switch places with Michael, but I made sure I was ready long beforehand. It's a good thing I did.

up and there he was! He had beaten his first half marathon time by thirteen minutes! I was so proud of him I could hardly contain myself. The smile on my face spread from ear to ear. Michael had to strap the Velcro computer-scoring chip around my leg and push me out onto the course!

Although he says he has no desire to complete a full marathon, I have a feeling he will surprise me again one of these days, and will trek the 26.2 miles by my side.

My name is Rhonda Kile. I've been running for over twenty years. I didn't start running until I was nearly thirty years old. I'll be fifty in January, and I plan to continue running well into my 80s, if not beyond! I've run five marathons, including London and Dublin. Michael and I reside in a suburb of South Bend, Indiana, with our two shelties, ages thirteen and fifteen, both retired runners.

The Real Race

I've been running for a long time. I started running when my mom read Kenneth Cooper's *The Aerobics Way*. She got jazzed about running a mile a day in under ten minutes and she dragged her kids along. I later ran on the track team in high school, and on those pre-Title IX days, also ran on the boys cross-country team. Since then, my running has waxed and waned, responding to the other things that life throws in.

I'm now forty-two and have two small children. I can't run six or seven-minute miles any more, and it's been more years than I can remember since I've broken a tape at a finish line. I try to do a 10K every year, but can't put a lot of miles in anymore. I'm the kind of runner who gets pooh-poohed by the faster, elite runners. They call me a "recreational" runner, or some other ridiculous term.

Recreational runner . . . hah! I learned a gazillion years ago that the REAL race is to keep running, even when you feel like you can't. It's true that the hardest part about going for a run is to get your shoes on. I'm overweight and not as shapely as I used to be, but I can still get out, pound the pavement, and come back knowing I've done something really good for myself. Running is one of the wonderful constants in my life that cures my blues, and gives me a remarkable sense of contentment that nothing else can. The incredible sense of well-being that comes with running is irreplaceable.

I figure maybe I can outlive the competition and maybe even start winning some races again when I get older!

My name is Lucienne Bouvier. I'm a forty-two year old married mother of two young sons, ages five and two. I'm an OB/GYN in Fremont, California.

Nothing is predestined:

The obstacles of your past

can become the gateways

that lead to new beginnings

— Ralph Blum

It's Never Too Late to Dream

When I was thirteen I had an older sister named Kathy whom I really admired. She ran track at her school. At age thirteen I was overweight and didn't have much self-esteem. One day while walking home from my grandparents' house, I imagined that I was running swiftly up a small incline on a gravel alley. I decided to actually try doing a short run. I felt heavy, slow and my legs hurt from the effort. But I kept running!

I had an old pair of tennis shoes, not running shoes, but they worked. Soon each shoe developed a hole on both sides. They were so bad that the soles separated from the shoes near the toes, so I used masking tape to hold them together. I wrapped the tape around and around my shoes. They were my very first "running" shoes from my first running days.

Every day I ran around a red dirt soccer field; sometimes I ran twice a day. I could do only two laps at a time, very slowly, but eventually I began to run longer. After three months I could do twelve laps altogether without stopping. This was a big thing for me. I told everyone in my family "I did twelve laps non-stop!" No one in my family thought I would stick with it, they thought running was a passing thing for me.

I ran all through my high school years, even running two marathons. I developed a deep love for running. During those days I used to run as many as fifteen to twenty-two miles a day. Unfortunately, once I entered adulthood, with all its problems, I stopped running and didn't run at all for twenty years. I even started smoking.

But deep inside I could still feel the memory of the way it felt when I ran as a child. At age thirty-six I met a wonderful friend, who became my husband. Because he was a runner, I used to ask him if he thought my running days were only memories. I asked him once, "Do you think I could still run after all these years, especially after all I've done to myself?" He said, "Cecelia, yes you can and it's not too late."

Those words started my journey back out into the sunshine, rain, and all kinds of weather to relive what I had lost for so many years. Eventually I stopped smoking and began to feel so much better about myself. At the age of forty-one, I have back that feeling I had so many years ago. I love running, I really do. I average fifty to seventy miles a week now, and I've done another marathon and two half-marathons in the past two years. I'm thankful to my husband, Douglas, who believed I could run again and to all the other runners I've come to know. I want to share my experience that it's never too late to dream, and to believe in those dreams. Running has returned me to a level I once thought was lost forever.

> Unfortunately, once I entered adulthood, with all its problems, I stopped running and didn't run at all for twenty years. I even started smoking.

Written by Cecelia La Pointe-Gorman
Tacoma, Washington

Take Nothing for Granted

I was running my first half-marathon. At the ten-mile mark, the sun came out and it started getting hot. I was tired and began to feel sorry for myself. It was so hot and my body was in pain.

Suddenly I heard a man's voice yelling, "Come on, you guys! Keep running! Good job!" I looked over to see who was cheering us on. There sat a homeless man in a wheelchair. He was clapping and waving as we ran by. As I looked at him I realized that he would give anything to feel my little pain.

It made me aware of how much we take for granted and what a wonderful thing it is to have the ability to get up every day and go for a run!

Written by Jennifer Lloyd-Hunt
Oceanside, California

The Day Elvis Died

My wife, Cathy, and I started running together the day Elvis Presley died. I would stop on our way home from work and run. At that time Cathy wasn't a runner; she would wait in the car for me while I ran. Cathy knew what a fan I was of Elvis, so as soon as she heard on the radio about his death, she ran to tell me.

> Cathy knew what a fan I was of Elvis, so as soon as she heard on the radio about his death she ran to tell me.

That started Cathy's love affair with running. We ran together for many years. I have stopped running due to injuries, but she continues to run four miles a day, seven days a week. We live in the Midwest, just outside of Kansas City, and the weather is not always good for running. People who complain about how cold or hot it is should see this five-foot, one-hundred-pound lady out there with a big grin on her face, enjoying her run! Cathy has been instrumental in getting more people interested in running than anyone I know. Everyone knows her as "that woman who's always running."

She has never had a running injury, although she fell last year on the ice and broke her wrist. That didn't stop her; she never missed a day. She did miss running one day when she broke her toe. When it happened she cried hard, not from the pain but because she thought she was going to have to stop running for a long time.

Cathy and I celebrated our thirty-second wedding anniversary on October 14, 2001. I can tell you without a doubt that running and physical fitness has played a major part in our marriage's longevity. Although I don't run anymore, I go to the gym and do yoga to stay in shape. There have been many nights I might not have gone if she would have missed her run to stay home with me. Cathy and I work together, so except for when she's running and J'm at the gym, we're always together. I can't remember the last time we had an argument. If we get cranky with each other, we go do our thing and come back with a different attitude. I'm so lucky to have her as my wife. You would like Cathy.

Cathy is fifty-one years old but no one believes it. She told me if she dies first she wants to be buried with her running shoes on. The worst possible thing I can imagine happening to her would be if she couldn't run. Cathy is a truly fine person, and a real runner. I love her very much.

My name is Larry Reid. Cathy and I live on a farm in Holt, Missouri, with our twenty-three cats, five dogs and five horses. We ran together every day for almost ten years until I injured my back and had to stop running.

Friend:

One who knows

all about you

and loves you just the same.

— Elbert Hubbard

Sharon & Shari's
Excellent Adventures

It all began at a 5K in a small town. We were two strangers with a common love of running. I was looking to increase mileage, with a marathon in mind. Shari was just looking to increase mileage. Little did we know how much that day would impact our lives. It was the birth of a life-changing relationship. Ten years and thirty-five marathons later (between us), we've had a few adventures along the road!

Neither of us ever imagined the inspiration and strength we would draw from our friendship. Over the years we've shared life experiences and every emotion from heart-wrenching sorrow to supreme joy. The therapeutic value of our friendship has been invaluable and a lot cheaper than professional counseling! We've solved the world's problems, discussed every frustration known to modern woman, planned our children's weddings, deepened our faith in God, planned meals, exchanged recipes, laughed until we cried, and achieved a decent level of fitness along the way!

After meeting and establishing our running partnership, our first big goal was to train for, and complete, a marathon. Schedules were discussed, plans made and training completed. Following a "feel good" approach — we laughed, sang and enjoyed our way to the finish in just over four hours — mission accomplished! That was only the beginning of our marathon saga.

Not known for sitting on our "laurels," we soon set new goals. The next year we would do better! Shari decided to qualify for Boston, while I was dubious. Nevertheless, we both ended up qualifying. We've had so many wonderful experiences over the years. One of the most outstanding occurred after the Disney Marathon. During a celebration lunch following the run, we met and talked with the late Fred Lebow, of New York City Marathon fame; we'll always cherish that memory. (We even had our photo taken with him.)

We attribute our running success to laughter and commitment. Knowing you have an appointment to run — it's harder to "wuss-out" because you're tired or it's raining/snowing/sleeting! Inevitably when we meet, we both agree that if it weren't for the other, we would have stayed in a toasty bed with a warm blanket and a good book!

> Inevitably when we meet, we both agree that if it weren't for the other, we would have stayed in a toasty bed with a warm blanket and a good book!

One run stands out. It was January 1996 and an icy winter blast had encased Northeast Pennsylvania. After weeks of heavy snow and ice, temperatures finally warmed to the fifties. Torrential rains brought floodwaters that overflowed the banks of the Susquehanna River. Small streams rushed over secondary roads, making many impassable.

On this particular day the howling winds and rain outside duplicated the unsettled emotions stirring within Shari. A family crisis seemed overwhelming. She wanted to huddle under the covers in a sea of denial and depression. Then I arrived for our regularly scheduled run. "Let's go! This is one you really need to do," I said. Lacking the strength to resist or argue, Shari donned her running gear, which included a water-repellent jacket, and we headed out the door and into the pouring rain.

The first few miles were miserable. The freezing rain shot icy pellets that stung our faces, and the frigid water on the roads began to seep into our shoes. Shari suppressed the not-so-serious urge to yell at me, while struggling to ignore all the emotions churning within her.

RUNNING FOR THE SOUL 2

Then the rapport between friends began to weave its magic. Healing words of encouragement and compassion, as well as a quiet prayer brought the miracle of healing. Peace engulfed Shari as she ran. We both share a deep and abiding faith in one who is greater than any challenge we might face.

Suddenly I glanced over at Shari and thought, "Oh, my gosh! She's foaming!" Shari's jacket was covered with white foam. As I was wondering what it might be, Shari looked down and saw the foam bubbling from her jacket. We looked at each other and burst out laughing.

It was then that Shari recalled the previous week's running conversation about needing a new washing machine. The old one didn't seem to be rinsing quite right — our run had confirmed that observation!

We continued on through icy water that covered our ankles sometimes because it was so deep. We received more than one warning from motorists that the road was nearly impassable. But on we ran. Finally, just before the turn-around point, we were forced to turn around as ice and water was flowing across the road. A road crew was out, and they watched incredulously as we sloshed through the icy rapids, laughing hysterically, leaving soap suds in our wake!

An emotional healing washed over us that day. Was it the words we had spoken, the astonished faces of the road crew, or the soap suds that washed away the gloom? No matter, the result was the same. Joy was restored and we had shared another fine escapade.

Who knows what waits for us in the future? Whatever it is, it will be better for having shared the experience.

My name is Sharon Templin. I'm an OB/GYN nurse, working in the Obstetrical Department at a hospital in Tunkhannock, Pennsylvania. Shari Philneck is a nursery school teacher at a Christian pre-school, also in Tunkhannock. Since we met ten years ago, we've completed many races and marathons, including seven Boston Marathons.

Let us move on and step out boldly,

though it be into the night

and we can scarcely see the way.

A Higher Intelligence than the mortal

sees the road before us.

— Charles B. Newcomb

More Than Just
Running Partners

I have been running for about fifteen months. When I started I weighed about two hundred twenty pounds and could only run one block. I ran one block and walked one and one-half blocks before I could breathe steadily enough to run another block.

I looked forward to each milestone. The next tree. One and one-half blocks. Two blocks. I remember the first time I ran a full mile: the excitement was truly amazing. I've been hooked ever since.

At the time I started running I knew only one other person who ran, my dearest friend, Tom. He would leave the office to run, and I couldn't imagine how he could get such pleasure from what seemed to me (at the time) to be such torture.

> He would leave the office to run, and I couldn't imagine how he could get such pleasure from what seemed to me (at the time) to be such torture.

Eventually Tom became my inspiration and motivation. Every time I conquered a new milestone, I ran to the phone to call him. His shared excitement was truly genuine. Our friendship has grown along the way. We share new milestones together now. We've become running partners as well as best friends. We run different speeds alone on the track, but we still have the ability to motivate and inspire one another. Now I run about five to six miles a day, four to six times a week; I almost always run with Tom.

Running has been a lifesaver for me. I'm now forty-five and weigh about one hundred sixty pounds.

I'm in the best physical shape of my life. I feel empowered after every run. I may begin my run with a lot on my mind, but at the end my mind is always at ease. There's no problem that a good run can't help me solve. This has been a difficult year for me. I'm truly convinced that if not for the power of running, it would have been even more difficult.

My name is Blanca I. Velez. I'm a forty-five year old Hispanic, divorcee and mother of two adult children. I'm probably the most optimistic person I know; I find the positive in every situation. I'm confident that something wonderful is in store for me in the very near future; I'm enthusiastic about the journey.

Running Is Inspirational
& a Family Affair

I say a prayer as I start each run. I ask God for strength, endurance and safety. Then I thank God for the ability to run.

Running never interested me until I hit forty. Then I started running on the local bike trail, called the Washington and Old Dominion (W&OD) Bike Trail. Running early in the morning is my favorite time — seeing a new day dawning. Running fits so well into God's creations: the sunrise, birds, deer, beavers and streams. My Dad died in 1996 and sometimes when I run I look up in the clouds and know he's looking down on me — he always loved nature.

Our family runs — not because they were forced to, but because they want to because Dad runs. One by one, each of our three children took up running with Dad. What a blessing it is to have your children run with you. We enjoy nature, talk and find ways to praise God while we run. Our oldest, Rick, went away to school in Chicago and ran the Chicago Marathon with a friend. Then, after he found out about the JFK 50-Miler in Maryland, he and his friend flew home for the weekend to run in that race. He even ran a 100-Miler right before he got married. Rick and I ran the Country Music Marathon in April 2001. He could have finished much faster, but he wanted to run and finish the race with his Dad — we crossed the finish line together.

> He could have finished much faster, but he wanted to run and finish the race with his Dad — we crossed the finish line together.

As I approach fifty, I thank God again that I can run. Even though I've had surgery and developed Type II diabetes during the past decade, I've still missed only one year of running. I'll never forget how I felt when I ran my first race in 1999. Tears were streaming down my face as I ran; I kept thinking, "Two years ago I didn't feel well enough to run, and today here I am running my first race."

My name is Bill Young; I'm an auditor for the U.S. Navy. I live in Leesburg, Virginia, with my wife, Donna. My three children are grown and out on their own. Rick and I finished the 2001 Marine Corps Marathon together.

SECTION III

HEALTH

You can do very little with faith,

but you can do nothing without it.

— Samuel Butler

The Beauty of a Quiet Sunrise

Fifteen months ago, at the tender age of fifty, I was diagnosed with cancer. Not a good thing. I've been a runner since my early twenties; I've completed two marathons (I have a personal best of 3:14) and many 10Ks. At the time of my diagnosis, I was running consistently eighteen to twenty miles a week. Fortunately, I was able to continue running nearly every day through four months of chemotherapy and forty-two days of radiation treatment. It wasn't easy! Chemo made me sick, but I dealt with it. Radiation was worse, I felt like a big siphon was sucking every bit of energy from my body and spirit.

I don't want to sound like I'm carrying on or acting proud, but I kept running because I was determined to maintain what had been a love in my life. Today, thanks to aggressive medicine, much faith, good conditioning and good luck, I'm in remission. This morning I ran five miles and enjoyed being alive and seeing the beauty of a quiet sunrise.

My name is Bruce Hillier, I live in Henderson, Nevada. I have a great family — a wonderful wife of twenty-nine years, four children and four grandchildren. A career mix of banking and domestic/international consulting has provided me the opportunity to hit the pavement in many interesting places. Today, I've traded airports and time zone changes for a more traditional career and time with family and friends.

Don't Worry about Me

On Saturday mornings, I wake up early, hop into my child-worn minivan and make my way to Lake Zurich High School, two towns over, and five miles away. Sometimes the sun is just barely rising over the trees, sometimes it's gray and raining. The weather never matters to me. As I turn onto the road that takes me to the school, I start to perk up in anticipation of what's ahead. People from around the area are gathering, all people just like me who've tumbled out of bed to go for a run. They're members of the Alpine Runners. Some are just out for a walk, others will jog and others will run fast because they're training for a race. On any given Saturday some will cover twenty or more miles, others three. I love that I get to hang out with these people — that's the best part. And I get to run.

I started running two years ago. My only other running came during a ten-week segment in gym class in the tenth grade. I don't remember that it was a bad experience, but once I met the requirement, I stopped running. As an adult, and the mother of three kids, I had become used to ignoring aches, pains and fatigue. But eventually the aches and pains began to worry me. I felt awful. If I felt like this at thirty-three, how could I look forward to being fifty, sixty or any older than I was?

So I went to my doctor. He ruled out all the scary possibilities, then went to work taking inventory. I had a minor slipped disk in my back and a benign cyst with some atrophy in my right quad. While treating my atrophied quad, I joined our town's community fitness center and started walking. Then I took aerobics classes and eventually added weights and cross-training equipment. The program also called for me to throw in five steps or so of jogging into every few minutes of walking. It hurt and I decided that I hated it. I whined enough that the instructor finally told me I didn't have to do it. So I stopped doing those terrible, not-for-me jogs for about a week or two, and felt much better.

When I saw runners on the street I admired them, but I always thought, "Me? Sweat like that? Put myself in that kind of pain?" It didn't sound like my kind of fun. Plus, I doubted I could be as cool as I thought I had to look to become a runner. In my mind, I was a dumpy, old housewife who had no business trying. And that was fine, because I didn't want to try. That might have been the end of it, but then the unthinkable happened.

On July 5, 1999, our park district held its annual 5K run and 1.5-mile fun walk. I really liked the staff at the fitness center, so to show support for them, and to get a T-shirt and goodie bag as credit for all the exercise I'd put myself through, my neighbor and I signed up for the walk. The walkers started shortly after the 5K began, and we walked an abbreviated race route. For the last half-mile or so, the routes came together. My neighbor and I chatted as we walked, and enjoyed

> In my mind, I was a dumpy, old housewife who had no business trying. And that was fine, because I didn't want to try.

the beauty of one of the older neighborhoods in our town. We chuckled because there were figures of runners on our T-shirts; we imagined that people would see us in them and think we actually ran the 5K.

As runners began to pass us I started noticing them. Some were parents of my children's friends. I had known they were runners, but I never thought they were frumpy, like me. I thought they were cool. I admired them. People who didn't look anything like runners began passing us. One man, who looked like he was in his sixties or seventies, passed us. We saw every age, shape and size of runner, both men and women. I thought that every last one of them was awesome. My idea of runners and what they look like changed during that race.

By the end of the morning I had it in my head that I wanted to run. I started jogging again every few steps while I was walking, and it didn't seem to hurt as much. I started joking with myself, wondering how I would ask my pain management and rehabilitation doctor if I could run. I figured he would say, "no."

When I saw the doctor three weeks later I told him about my "near-race experience" and my new-found desire to run a 5K by the following summer. That was all I figured I'd ever be able to do, just a dare of sorts, a few minutes of glory for attempting such a feat and succeeding, not for speed. And I really wanted another T-shirt! The doctor put me on a treadmill and said, "Yes, Shannon, you can learn to run three miles." I was thrilled!

> We saw every age, shape and size of runner, both men and women. I thought that every last one of them was awesome. My idea of runners and what they look like changed during that race.

But there was more. He kept on talking. He said that not only did he think I'd be able to run three miles within the year, but that I'd probably even learn to enjoy the experience.

Then he said, ". . . and if you think that's fun, just wait . . . there's so much more!" At that point I became both panicky and thrilled. He was treating me not like the crazy person I secretly thought I was for wanting to run, but like a person about to embark on a great journey. He told me about all the 5Ks in the Chicago area. He told me about 10Ks! Half-marathons! Marathons! He told me that I was not too old to start and that many marathon runners are in their prime at my age. Then he told me about Sister Marion Irvine, who qualified for the Olympic Marathon Trials at the age of fifty-four. Wow! I had no idea that such a world existed — a world of runners. Masses of runners, some like me, some like Sister Irvine, some like the doctor who was so enthusiastic about running (and work). It was quite an awakening.

He talked more — about training logs, heart rate monitors, stress tests, and marathon training. All the while he was talking I kept thinking, "Why, he's talking to me like an athlete; me, the kook." Over the years I've retained much of what he

> Then he told me about Sister Marion Irvine, who qualified for the Olympic Marathon Trials at the age of fifty-four.

told me. I now have many race T-shirts and I've met so many other enthusiastic, encouraging people. When I think about them all, I can't help but smile.

Now I get excited for anyone I meet who wants to learn to run. I want them to feel like they are doing something awesome, because they are. I tell them that they can succeed, they aren't alone. I tell them, "If you think three miles is cool . . . just wait!" Running has given me more than I ever expected. I'm learning to take care of myself. I'm learning how good it feels to challenge myself and succeed. And I'm discovering how much fun it is to become part of the running community. I've also learned that it's OK to make time for myself, and to savor the quiet moments when I run on my own.

Running has also overflowed into my family life. At first my husband worried because he thought I'd get hurt and become as miserable as I'd been before I sought medical help. I worried because I feared running might take me away from my husband and children too much. Then my husband started worrying that I might go completely nuts and try to run a marathon — and get hurt. Well, I'm training for a marathon now and plan on running my first one this fall. Since I've evolved into a long-distance runner, it seems like a reasonable challenge. Nobody's worried about me.

I've met many wonderful people because I wanted to learn to run three miles. I continue to have terrific adventures. I'm not a speed demon. I don't look like an Olympian. I don't care anymore. I'm just happy to be here. And I'm still amazed at how we runners swap our stories, challenge ourselves and support one another. Of course, there are also people in my life who aren't runners or athletes, but they support me, listen to me and encourage me. They may very well be the most important part of my adventure. Life is good. I'm reminded of that on Saturday mornings, while my family is snug in their beds, as I head to the high school to run in the rain.

Written by Shannon Daab
Mundelein, Illinois

Challenges make you

discover things about yourself

that you never really knew.

They're what make the

instrument stretch, what

make you go beyond the norm.

— Cicely Tyson

There are times in everyone's life

when something constructive

is born out of adversity . . .

when things seem so bad that

you've got to grab your fate by

the shoulders and shake it.

— Anonymous

The Heart of My Story

I started running in 1984 after I was involved in a car accident. My blood pressure was very high and since I was quite heavy, the doctor told me to lose weight. He said that the best way to lose weight was to take up running. So I did. The weight started to come off, but something else happened as well, and this is the heart of my story.

For many years I had suffered from deep bouts of depression because I felt guilty that I had survived Vietnam. Granted, I hadn't seen the action that many others had, but two of my friends had died there, one was my best friend from back home. Another had his legs nearly blown off in front of me by one of our own booby traps. The depression was bad enough that it affected my life in many ways.

When I started running (and losing weight), I began to notice that my bouts of depression were of much shorter duration, and I wasn't having them as often. I started to feel better about myself and my whole life began to change. Finally the depression completely disappeared, as did my feelings of guilt. During my runs, I realized the answer to the question I had been seeking for so many years; "Why did I survive and my friends die or were maimed?" I know now that there is no answer, so it's fruitless to seek one. Today I run because I love doing it and I enjoy those benefits that go far beyond losing weight and lowering blood pressure.

Written by Luis Arauz
Fresh Meadows, New York

No Couch Potato Here

I'm seventy-three years of age and I started running when I was fifty-three. Running has helped me keep my sanity at several times in my life. When I've had depressing things happen, I've found that if I go out and run a few miles, I come back home and mentally feel much better. Now that I'm older, it's harder, but I keep doing the best I can. I don't worry much about my time; just to be able to run is the most important thing. Health-wise, I'm much better off than someone who has been a coach potato, and for this I'm very thankful.

> **I'm seventy-three years of age and I started running when I was fifty-three.**

My name is Marie Alderman. I live in Morehead City, North Carolina (at the beach), and I'm seventy-three years young. I'm not running as much as I did in the past, but mentally I'm still there. Once you become a runner, you never lose the desire to continue. I have many age-group medals, probably more than 125. I've enjoyed all my races and I've made many friends.

Photographs Don't Lie

I've always been a runner — the problem is that I'm forty-one and I hadn't run in thirty years. I don't know how a person can end up in such horrid physical condition. It's denial at best. One day I looked at a photograph and couldn't figure out who that sad-looking fat man was sitting next to my wife. I didn't think I was too bad until I saw that photo — when I looked at it I realized that I had to do something if I wanted to live another five years. At the time I stood 5'6" and weighed 225. I would break a sweat just getting dressed. Sometimes after I had showered and dried off, I would be soaked again by the time I was dressed.

So I decided that I would start to eat right and run again. In nine months I went from 225 pounds down to 160, and I plan on losing ten or fifteen more. My waist used to be forty-two inches, now it's thirty-two and I've had to buy a whole new wardrobe.

While my weight and appearance is important, what matters most to me is how I feel about myself in general. I know now that I'm strong and can accomplish my goals. I run every day — running is part of my life and who I am. The feelings of control, freedom and self-worth I get from running are more powerful than the human desire to do nothing — it will always be that way for me, I know it. I'm running the Chicago Marathon in 2002 and I will always be thankful for the drive and motivation that this sport has given me.

My name is Rick Adams. I live in Middlebury, Indiana, with Sandy, my wife of nineteen years. I have three children. In my spare time I run, bike, fish and play the guitar.

My Zen

In September 1999 I split up with my husband of sixteen years (my decision) and struck out on my own. I can honestly say that I lost my way for about a year and a half. In October 2000 I lost my mother to colon cancer; she had been still young to me and she went so quickly. At the time I was smoking cigars and not taking care of myself at all. I wasn't exercising, I was drinking more than I should and eating fast foods. Had I chosen to run and exercise during this very stressful period of my life, I would have had an easier time dealing with it. I had always been very athletic, but I had let myself go. I would feel so guilty when I saw runners, walkers or bikers go by, knowing it could be me, but I chose otherwise.

I made a decision in February 2001 to quit smoking. I told myself I didn't want to be smoking when I turned forty-one, so I quit on February 1st and never smoked again. Eventually I started exercising again, first on a treadmill and rowing machine and then when the weather got better, I moved outside to the fresh air and elements. I began running slowly in a populated area at 5:00 AM, so no one would see me struggling to coordinate my breathing and running. Finally, I graduated to twenty minutes every morning, except weekends.

Due to a family history of cancer, I had a complete hysterectomy on May 10, 2001. During the six weeks following surgery all I thought about was when I could start running again. Now that my recuperation is over, I'm running 5Ks and 10Ks. Running has always been my Zen.

Written by Kelly Reid
Millington, Tennessee

Keeping My Center

Approximately two and one-half years ago I was diagnosed with Attention Deficit Disorder. On the one hand, the diagnosis was a relief because there was a name for the fog I had been in as long as I could remember, and there was medication to address my condition. The problem was that the medication only took me so far. I realized that in order to cope with my situation, the rest was going to be up to me.

I began looking back to my past to determine the period in my life when I had felt the most clarity of mind. I remembered that during college, when I was most stressed out, I would go out for a run. I never considered it as physical exercise. I went to the gym for that. I needed to take my mind out for a run and lose myself in thoughts.

Once I realized what running did for my mind, I rediscovered running. Running has brought new clarity to my life. I run three to four times a week for about an hour or so. I run early in the morning, preferably in the dark and always alone. There's something incredibly empowering about running. For that three to four hours a week, I'm the master of my own universe. My running is my time, period. I wouldn't trade it for the world.

> For that three to four hours a week, I'm the master of my own universe. My running is my time, period. I wouldn't trade it for the world.

Running has also done wonders for my self-esteem and it puts me in sync with my body and mind, during and after my run. I've been able to accomplish a lot, and I owe it primarily to running. Racing has taught me both patience and that I can reach any goal I set and train for. I also believe that the discipline of running religiously has carried over into my personal and professional life. I'm a trial attorney, and I find that when I'm in a trial, I run like crazy. Running is what keeps me centered.

I look forward to running for many years. Regardless of whether it makes me live longer or not, the quality of life that running has given me makes it well worth it.

My name is Robert Tudisco. I live with my wife and son in Eastchester, New York.

There is no genius in life

like the genius of energy and activity.

— Donald G. Mitchell

SECTION IV

WISDOM

The only measure of what you believe

is what you do.

If you want to know

what people believe,

don't read what they write,

don't ask them what they believe,

just observe what they do.

— Ashley Montagu

The Curves in the Road

I reached beyond the bassinet and the nine-pound pink bundle, for the book on the bedside table. I had just given birth to my third child and I was about to start reading *The Non-Runners Marathon Trainer*. Was I crazy or had the drugs from my c-section not worn off yet? I was completely in love with my little girl, and my other young children (ages three and one) waiting for me at home, but I needed a goal, some motivation, a PLAN! This training manual was it!

Over the next few months as I made my way through the pages, I began to log the miles. Even though I had never run much more than a 10K, with each long run I felt stronger and closer to my goal. My initial plan was to lose a little baby weight and get back in shape, but the road quickly became my obsession, my drug of choice. I would head out of the house at 5:30 AM to selfishly rely on my only free sixty minutes of the day. It was my hour to run, not to be a mom or a wife. Not to clean faces, change diapers, put on shoes or explain why mommies need time alone, too! My goal was the 1999 Chicago Marathon.

I was on track and ready to go, mentally and physically. Then, four days before the marathon, I found out I was pregnant!

As October got closer, the long runs reached seventeen, eighteen and then twenty miles. I was on track and ready to go, mentally and physically. Then, four days before the marathon, I found out I was pregnant! The training book had given me lots of suggestions on "what if?" situations to help would-be marathoners. Advice on how to handle possible road blocks on the journey to completing 26.2 miles, but nowhere did the book mention how

to deal with this! Shocked, joyful and sad, I discussed the situation with my doctor and was
cleared to run. I completed the marathon in 4:44,
and gave birth to a healthy fourth child eight months
later. My "marathon" baby always reminds me
that it's good to plan for your journey ahead, but
sometimes it's the curves in the road that we least
expect that keep life interesting and renew our
joy of running!

*My name is Erin Phillips. I've been married to my best friend for
ten years. We have four incredible children who keep me running
on and off the road. We live in the small Iowa town of Pella.*

Our nature consists of motion;

complete rest is death.

— Blaise Pascal

The Meaning of Cross-Country

I always wanted to go to the United States, so I went for one year as a foreign exchange student. Somehow, while I was there, I became a cross-country runner. The fact that I was fascinated by the words "cross-country," is one of the reasons why I got involved with the sport. My goal became to make it to every single practice, every day, because I knew if I started missing out on the training it would become a habit.

This year has been a challenging one for me, and I've had many difficult situations to deal with. Running has given me strength to face the challenges, and it has helped me to start believing in myself. Now I know that I can achieve much more than I ever thought possible. I was always the kind of person who would get angry and unhappy when bad things happened; it's unbelievable how much I've changed. I still have the same kind of personality, but I have so much more patience and ambition.

Running is like therapy. It's something that's between only my body and my will. When times are hard, I know I can always go out for a run. I achieved a lot in my "Running America Year." I wish for everybody to find the same passion for something in his or her life. You'll be a better person for it, and if you don't do it, no one will do it for you.

That's what I learned from running. It's now part of my life. Thanks, cross-country (even though I must admit, at first I thought those runners were a little strange!)

Written by Jane Hingst
Freiburg, Germany

Bell Lap

As runners, we all know what's meant by "the bell lap": that final ring that resonates through us all. By that point in a race, we know that there's a limit in us somewhere, but it's up to us to decide how far we're going to push it.

In previous races, I've always heard the bell lap from some other place on the track. It has always symbolized in my mind the pain that comes with finishing a tough race. When the bell rings, every muscle in my body tenses, my eyes narrow, and I can almost feel the adrenaline hitting my bloodstream. That's how it's always been, until today.

Today I had control over when the bell rang. Rang so every one of my competitors heard it. In a way, I created the pain for them that comes with trying to catch the elusive bell-ringer. Even though this race wasn't my best time, I feel the exhilaration of achieving something I've never done before. And although I feel a little sorry for causing other runners pain, I know that's what competing is all about. If not for those moments when you give all you've got and it still isn't enough, there wouldn't be those moments when you feel unbelievably happy, yet totally drained physically. I call it blissful exhaustion.

There's always a lesson to be learned from running, and the bell lap taught me how to love and hate running at the same time. From here on out, it's all bittersweet.

My name is Eleanor Lehnert. I'm a seventeen-year-old senior at Kingsford High School in Iron Mountain, Michigan. I run both cross-country and track and also enjoy kayaking and camping. I hope to become a doctor.

Slowing Down

Up until a few years ago, I hated to run. I mean, I really hated it. I think it was because I had to run laps in elementary school, and I was always the slowest kid to finish. I did everything in my power to avoid it. That is, until I joined the U.S. Navy.

They run you into the ground in boot camp, and they don't care if you hate to run. They don't care if you like to run. You just run, and run and run.

It was after boot camp that I decided that running wasn't such a bad thing. Why then? you might wonder. Well, in boot camp you have no privacy, no quiet time of your own. You eat when they want you to eat, think what they want, and sleep when they want. Running was the only time when you can be alone with your thoughts.

OK, so I was still the slowest person running around the track, but on the backside where there were no drill instructors, it was awfully nice. It made me want to run slower so I could savor the moment.

You know when you get to the point in your run when your brain shuts down and you can hear nothing at all that it's going to be a good day? I still run, even though there's no one making me and there's no incentive or promotion depending on it. I run simply to run.

I'm still the slowest person out there, but you know what? Everyone needs to slow down once in a while.

My name is Bernadette Gallagher. I live in San Diego, California, with my husband, Paul, and two dogs, Ben and Duncan.

I am not bound to win,

but I am bound to be true.

I am not bound to succeed,

but I am bound to

live up to what light I have.

— Abraham Lincoln

Another Kind of Hero

A cold wind blew the golden leaves across the hard ground. They made a rasping sound, like a death rattle. The sound matched his breathing — harsh, grating and painful. Sweat, frozen in crystal crust at the end of his hair, flopped each time he took another stride. His feet fell heavily on the ground. He wore tattered sneakers, shredded from the millions of small pebbles he'd run through. His sweatpants were gray. The color matched his complexion. His arms flopped in exhaustion, like flowers that sway when giving in to a cold winter wind.

He was what most would consider a lost cause. There are no winners or losers; it isn't even a game. To others it looks as if he's doing something for no reason. No one can see him. He could break a world record that no one would even see, pointless. His legs screamed at him to stop. His scorched lungs pleaded for rest. Even his socks seemed to fly at half-mast around his ankles — soiled flags of surrender. Still, he ran.

In the autumn of our dreams, we are all quarterbacks. We are cunning and graceful and when we step into the huddle, everyone bends forward eagerly. The crowd rises expectantly because they know we will deliver the victory just as the clock blinks down to zero. Ah . . . but that's the autumn of our dreams, not the winter of our reality.

You want to know about reality? Then go watch the "other" autumn sport. It's called cross-country. Watch it and you will know what they mean when they speak of the loneliness of the long-distance runner.

Cross-country runners don't get championship rings, MVP trophies or offers to endorse deodorant or fancy cars. Cross-country runners get shin splints, blisters on their feet, runny noses, watery eyes and painful cramps. There's no crowd, no cheerleaders, just the hard ground and ugly trees with no leaves. A guy driving by in a car, honking his horn, grinning like a clueless jerk. What cross-country runners do get is a special kind of self-satisfaction that few of us are ever privileged to experience. It's not from winning, it's merely from finishing. It's going out on a chilly, dark afternoon to stand on the starting line. It's running through puddles and muddy spots. It's going up hills and down hills, all the while telling lies to your legs. It's the ability to keep on running when others pass you, sometimes right at the end. The ability to keep running is having the guts deep inside you to give it your all. That, my friends, is reality.

People get all caught up in the flash, slam-dunks, power-play goals and home runs. Sometimes they get the notion that what happens to some over-the-hill, drug addicted, millionaire baseball legend ranks right up there in importance with the Dead Sea Scrolls. So, they tend to dismiss cross-country as a "minor" sport. Besides, who knows how to read a stopwatch past the four-minute mark, anyway? The only time they care about running is once every four years at the Olympics.

Sometimes they get the notion that what happens to some over-the-hill, drug addicted, millionaire baseball legend ranks right up there in importance with the Dead Sea Scrolls.

So, in our fantasies, the hero is the guy who scores the winning touchdown. But that's not reality. Reality is the kid you see when you're driving through an abandoned park or past a snowy track. He's the kid with the stocking cap and the sweat-stained shirt, loping along for no apparent reason. His eyelids flickering wildly, in a hypnotic trance of pain and determination contorting his face.

Maybe he won't be able to put into words why he runs. Maybe he'll mention something about "gutting it out" or pushing through the pain barrier or running because he has this internal drive to discover just how much he's capable (or not capable) of. That can be the harshest kind of reality. Anyone who's willing to confront it, is, in the truest, purest sense, not just an athlete but another kind of hero.

My name is Zach Emerson. I'm a distance runner from Hillsboro-Deering High School in Hillsboro, New Hampshire. I love to run. It's by far my favorite thing to do. I'll keep running as long as I have my legs and my heart.

Ex Wanna Be Pom-Pom Girl

I remember the unusually hot spring afternoon like it was yesterday. I was wearing a too-big-for-me pair of black shorts and a short-sleeved knit sweater from my mom's closet. I still had braces on my teeth and my haircut was anything but trendy. But I wasn't thinking about my less-than-cool status or my look. I was thirteen years old, and terribly nervous and excited about trying out for the eighth-grade cheerleading team. How I dreamed of being a cheerleader! Wearing a short skirt and school sweater, finally fitting in at school . . . I could only imagine.

Twenty-one girls were called up and I was first. First! I had no idea what to do. I needed to watch a few other girls to get the hang of it, to see what the judges were looking for. But I was called first and one week later when the meeting was held to announce the results, I learned that I had blown it. I wasn't chosen. No short skirt, football games along the sidelines, invites out with the "in" crowd. Deflated, I walked down the hall with my head down, wondering what I should do. When I looked up, I saw a sign straight ahead on the gymnasium door that read "cross-country meeting — 3 PM today." Cross-country? What did I have to lose? The new cheerleaders were already outside practicing their cartwheels and cheers, and I had nothing better to do except for an English assignment, so why not?

I opened the gym door and took a seat with about fifteen other kids. Our art teacher, clad in running shorts, T-shirt and tennis shoes, introduced himself as our school's new cross-country coach. He gave us a schedule, and told us to meet in the gym again the next day, wearing some comfortable running shoes.

Well, I'll bet you can already guess that being on the cross-country team was, in hindsight, a much better fit for me than making the cheerleading team anyway. That first season I set the junior high girl's record in the 2.1-mile race, running a time of 18:34 and ended up running cross-country for three more seasons. I ran a total of six seasons in track. Although I didn't run on a cross-country team in college, I continued to run on my own. In October 2000 I ran my first marathon, with my fiancée, also an avid runner. I've recently started training for a triathlon. Today I run four times a week, including long runs on the weekends.

Do I regret never owning a set of pom-poms? Not a chance!

The braces are gone and thanks to good eating habits and consistent running, I haven't gained a pound since high school. Running takes away the stress after a long day at work, keeps me in great shape, and is a wonderful way for me to spend time with my soon-to-be-husband. Do I regret never owning a set of pom-poms? Not a chance!

My name is Traci Dalton. I live in Columbus, Ohio, with my fiancée, Scott. I was a Peace Corps volunteer in Zimbabwe before working in the inner cities of Chicago and Cleveland as a public librarian.

In all human affairs

there are efforts,

and there are results,

and the strength of the effort

is the measure of the result.

— James Lane Allen

Don't Sweat It

On the way to my regional cross-country meet last year, I didn't know how I was going to do. Since I was in the eighth grade, this was my first year on the team. I tried to stay focused on finishing 15th place or better. The girls raced first, so I had a little more time to think about the race and stretch out and warm up. All the girls finished and the guys walked over to the start line. I was so nervous. I heard the gun go off and I thought, "go, go, go." It was a fast start, my fastest of the season. I thought, "I can't stay on this pace." I passed the one-mile mark in 6:10. I was starting to get really tired. I passed the two-mile mark in 11:54, which meant I had run a 5:44 mile. I picked up the pace a lot. I came around the tennis and basketball courts at an all-out sprint, with a tenth of a mile to go. I sprinted as hard as I could. It hurt so much, but I did it. I hit a root or something and tripped up, but didn't fall and the boy who had been behind me the whole race passed me then. Before I tripped and he passed me, I had been in 15th place. After he passed me, I started to sprint as hard as I could, but I couldn't catch him. I crossed the finish line in 18:12, in 16th place. I was so mad. But I felt better when I found out that I was still going to State, along with the rest of the guys and the whole girls' team. At that meet I learned that you have to work very hard if you want to achieve a goal. And if you don't achieve your goal, don't make such a big deal about it 'cause you'll achieve it sometime.

My name is Patrick Beckman. I'm fourteen. I'm a ninth grader at James Island High School in Charleston, South Carolina. I've been running for a year and a half.

Character

cannot be developed

in ease and quiet.

Only through experience of

trial and suffering can

the soul be strengthened,

vision cleared,

ambition inspired,

and success achieved.

— Helen Keller

SECTION V

LOVE

Miracles occur naturally

as expressions of love.

The real miracle is

the love that inspires them.

In this sense, everything

that comes from love is a miracle.

— A Course in Miracles

For Peyton

I have always been a runner. Mostly I've run for the health benefits. The longest I had ever run was a half-marathon, but in the summer of 2000 I started talking about running a full marathon with my running group. We could hardly imagine running for that long.

My wife was pregnant with our second child at the time, so the idea kind of came and went. On June 21, 2000, our son, Peyton, was born at only twenty-two weeks' gestation. He lived eight hours and passed away due to complications of his premature birth. The loss was devastating to my wife and me. We looked for ways to cope with our grief.

I began to lose myself in running, so much so that I decided to train for and run the Mardi Gras Marathon in New Orleans, and dedicate it to the memory of my son. I've always been the kind of person who sets a goal and doesn't stop until it's achieved. However, this goal felt out of my reach. But I persevered, found a sixteen-week training schedule and got started.

As I ran I could feel all my emotions intensify. I'd run faster and faster to relieve anger. I'd run long and slower so I could think. Sometimes I'd cry while I ran. I read a marathon training article that suggested creating a saying to use during your long runs when you felt tired, or when you started to feel "the wall" creeping up on you. Coming up with a saying was easy.

As I ran I'd say to myself, "I am running for Peyton, and I will not fail." I became obsessed with running and didn't miss a day. My wife was the only person who knew why I was running. This quest was between my son and me.

The day of the marathon, February 4, 2001, came quickly. The two-hour ride to New Orleans seemed to take forever. As I waited before the race, I was very nervous. If I didn't make it, I'd be letting down both my son and myself. I started thinking about my longest training run, a twenty-miler, and how I'd barely made it. As I lined up for the start I reflected on Peyton and the eight hours he was with us. I was wearing a pin on my shirt that Peyton had been given clipped to a stuffed animal. I looked at it for a while and realized that I was running for him and I would not fail.

The starting gun went off and as the mass of runners began to slowly move toward the start, I had to fight back tears. I tried to think of pacing and running smart, but all I could think of was Peyton. My running group was there to run the half-marathon, so I ran with them for the first ten miles and let them set the pace. In my head I relived the day my son was born and the events leading up to his death. I was running well and I felt good.

At mile twenty I hit the wall. My pace slowed and all I wanted to do was walk. I started to repeat "I am running for Peyton and I will not fail." At mile twenty-one I started to spell his name. I went numb and all I could hear was myself saying, "I will not fail" over and over again as I spelled his name.

> At mile twenty-five my body made me stop and walk. I walked about fifty feet and began to feel the overwhelming disappointment of not finishing.

At mile twenty-five my body made me stop and walk. I walked about fifty feet and began to feel the overwhelming disappointment of not finishing. I said to myself, "Oh, hell no! You've come this far and you will finish for Peyton." I started to run again and refused to stop. As I entered the Super-dome and saw the finish line I couldn't even hear the crowd.

I crossed the finish line in 4:33. I was disoriented for a short time and walked in circles for a few minutes. My body was screaming at me, every muscle was cramping and tight. It wasn't until the ride home that I felt the satisfaction of finishing. I knew that Peyton had been with me as I struggled over those last few miles. I couldn't have finished without him.

A few days later I went to his grave and placed my finisher medallion around the headstone. I realize now that this was such a healing event in my life. I do not feel the anger and am at peace with God.

They say you never forget your first marathon. I know this will be very true for me. No matter how much faster I run or how much harder the course, nothing will ever live up to the marathon that Peyton and I shared.

> A few days later
> I went to his grave
> and placed my
> finisher medallion
> around the headstone.

My name is Paul Kostmayer. I am a thirty-year-old critical care RN in Biloxi, Mississippi. I married my high school sweetheart, Shereen, and we have one beautiful daughter, Micaela (who is three and can run a mile.) I have been running races for fifteen years and have run three more marathons since the one I shared with my Peyton. I'm happy to share my story of self-healing.

The most important

single influence

in the life of a person

is another person . . .

who is worthy of emulation.

— Paul D. Shafer

A Father's Legacy

My Dad had gone through some terrible cancer surgery, so I went to see him. Dad had changed from a Golden Glove boxer in the Army to a breathing skeleton sitting in a chair, barely moving.

Because I had recently qualified for the Sheppard AFB running championships, I had to train during my visit. Every day I would sit with him, then go out for a run. After three days of seeing me leave to run, dad began to ask questions. When I arrived for our visit the next day, dad had his shoes on and when he saw me he said, "Let's go." We got four steps out the door and I had to carry him back to his chair.

This routine continued on for several days, and by the end of the first week he could make it to the curb. Two weeks later he was up to walking one block. Back home by then, I kept thinking about the effort he was putting out as I continued to train for my championship race. Two weeks out from my race my mom called to tell me that dad was walking a mile every day.

Race day came. All the qualifiers lined up and as I looked around I saw that many were much younger people from various branches of the service. For a fleeting second I wondered why I was there. The gun went off and the runners surged. I suddenly knew why I was there; I felt good and stayed in the top ten as we rounded the first lap of the track. We hit the street and people began to move around a little. My race was going very well. The finish line was now only one-half mile away. The pack was still fairly tight. The first-place runner was in a league of his own and everyone knew he would defend his title. Eight runners separated me from him. I picked up speed and started passing them, one by one. With a quarter-mile to go, there were only three runners between me and the lead runner.

I gazed ahead to the fast-approaching finish line and there stood my dad! His blue, baggy pajamas waving in the breeze and big smile lighting up his face. He was leaning against a tree beyond the finish line. That was all I needed. I hit another gear, passed the last few runners and finished second. I sped back to the tree and my dad was gone, that quick.

> His blue, baggy pajamas waving in the breeze, and big smile lighting up his face. He was leaning against a tree beyond the finish line. That was all I needed.

I run for many reasons. One is because I can. I also do it for those who aren't able to. The last five years my running has been a series of frustrating events. My hero is dead. My mentor and his inspiration seem to be hiding far away. Still, in my mind I visit my dad regularly. It was only recently that I came to realize that he's not as far away as I thought. His race has been done for a while, but he's really still here and would like me to do this for myself now.

My name is Dan Pengilly. I'm forty-four years old and I live in San Angelo, Texas. I have several goals I want to accomplish before I'm done. First is to run a sub-40 minute 10K. Second, finish a 100-mile race. And when I'm 89, to enter and win my age group in a 10K.

He alone is great

who turns the voice of

the wind into a song

made sweeter by his own loving.

— Kahil Gibran

Leaving

Every parent knows they will face the day when their children leave them. It might be physical, such as going away to college or moving out of the house, or it might be psychological, as the maturing child distances himself emotionally.

If you and your child are runners, however, the leaving process might take another tact. In my case, since I was never very fast to start with and could only hope to not slow down too quickly, I realized that my son, Adam, would be leaving me soon . . . in a running sense.

From the day five-year-old Adam ran his first 5K with me on Father's Day, I knew the inevitable would come sooner rather than later. Adam was fast, and had endurance. He would only get better. Time was Adam's ally — it was my enemy.

During the next few years we ran many races together, mostly 5Ks, but occasionally a five-miler or 10K, as well. We ran together, each of us wearing an identical shirt from a previous race. Tacky, yes, but some of my proudest memories are rekindled by the photographs I have of us running together in our matching outfits.

Then finally it happened. There was no warning. Race day came just like any other. It was a local 5K we had done in the past, with a steep uphill at the start, then a downhill that flattened out for the last half-mile.

> We ran together, each of us wearing an identical shirt from a previous race. Tacky, yes, but some of my proudest memories are rekindled by the photographs I have of us running together in our matching outfits.

We slowly started up the hill. There were a couple of kids ahead of us. I had to hold Adam back from charging up after them.

As we crested the hill, we saw the leading boys at the water stop. While they stopped to drink and get their breath back, we passed them in a rush. Now it was downhill for a mile and Adam and I lengthened our strides and let gravity do its thing. As we flew down the hill, I worried about the boys behind us, who had taken off like shots when they saw Adam pass them. I worried about our pace, whether Adam would burn out when we hit the flat half-mile before the finish. I needn't have worried.

We rounded the corner at the bottom of the hill and could see the finish up ahead. I looked back to see the boys not far behind us, seemingly closing the gap with every stride. I told Adam they were coming up, and asked him if he felt OK. That was it. He took off as if he had jets on his feet instead of running shoes. I panicked since I figured he couldn't possibly keep running so fast for the last half-mile. And the other boys had passed me. I tried to keep an eye on Adam to see if he could hold them off, but I lost him in the crush of runners. He was, after all, less than five feet tall.

Eventually he started coming back to meet me after he had finished his race, to run the last mile or so with me as a cool down. I never knew whether to laugh or cry.

Finally, as I chugged along, I saw him at the finish. He had kept up his pace. He had held off the other boys. He had run away from me. I was so proud. I was so upset.

That was the last race we would run together. Oh, we still ran many of the same races, but Adam was now getting faster and faster. I, on the other hand, was not. Eventually he started coming back to meet me after he had finished his race, to run the last mile or so with me as a cool down. I never knew whether to laugh or cry.

We actually did run one more race together. It was in Walt Disney World, where I was running a marathon and Adam was running his first half-marathon. He stayed with me for the first three miles, but I knew my pace was way too slow for him. He kept slowly pulling away, would realize what he had done and would wait for me to catch him. Finally, I called him over, kissed him and told him to go have fun.

There were tears in my eyes as I watched my son run away from me again. As a runner, he had left me for the final time.

Brian and Adam Henry were each born in the New York City area, where they both started running in the late 1980s. They ran their first races on the same day in 1990, where Adam showed what was to come by winning his children's race that day. Brian finished his 10K in a vertical position.

They ran their last race together in Walt Disney World in 1999, although they each plan on running there again in 2002, but not together.

Now living in Arizona, Brian likes to blame the heat for his incredibly increasing race times. Adam, now 16, has added multi-sports to his resume, qualifying in 2000 for the U.S. National Junior Duathlon team. He is unaffected by the heat.

Spirit Imbued

I began my morning run in the wee hours of a lovely summer day where I live, in the heart of the East Village in Manhattan. As I ran through the winding, desolate streets, I felt a certain peace wash over me, like a warm afternoon rain. Tranquility filled my being as I continued on my journey.

Traveling along at a quick, steady pace, I felt the presence of someone else. My Grandfather's spirit filled my mind and body, and carried me through the difficult hills of Central Park.

As I made my way out of the park, I quietly thanked my Grandfather for visiting me on that particular day, and helping me through a long training run. Sometimes we need a person, or a spirit, to push us along when we feel like a "lone wolf." We human beings need one another, if not in this world alone . . .

Laurie Meacham resides, writes and runs in New York City. She has been a runner since the age of nine. Her favorite race is the marathon. She ran her PR of 3:11:32 at the Boston Marathon in April 2001.

When Melissa Waves

I'm a high school special education teacher. June 6, 1996 (my 37th birthday), started out like any other school day. There were still a few weeks left in the semester and I was ready for school to end. About 1:00 PM I received a call from a co-worker who told me that Melissa had not reported to her worksite; she wanted to know if Melissa was with me. About the same time I noticed a lot of commotion going on at the school: an ambulance and police had arrived and administrators were walking around the building looking frantic.

One of my senior boys had lured Melissa into the woods by the school during lunch and stabbed her over forty times. Then he asked one of the younger students for help in getting himself cleaned up and rode the bus to his worksite. Melissa had died within minutes. The student was arrested.

When I got home from school that day, I didn't know what to do. I just wanted to go out for my afternoon run. I had been running for about a year, but never a lot of mileage. That day I just kept running and thinking and tried to sort things out in my head.

The last two weeks of school were very difficult. I had to help co-workers, fifteen special education students and myself deal with grief, guilt and Melissa's funeral. Every day I would go home and run and think. Running helped my stress; it helped me appreciate how lucky I was to have what I did.

Once school was out I began running by Melissa's grave. A student had placed a pinwheel on her burial place the day of the funeral. It seemed as though that pinwheel was always blowing, as though Melissa were waving at me. I kept adding mileage that summer and a few years later I completed my first marathon. Recently I finished my second. Being a teacher of high school special education students can be very rewarding, but very stressful. I always look forward to going home after school and getting out there and just running. Running off the stress, no matter the weather — I'm out there. So many people say to me: "Oh, how do you do it? You're so patient with those kids." My reply: "I run!"

My name is Maria DeRado. I was never athletic in high school — in fact I didn't start running until I was about thirty-five. I'm not a fast runner and probably never will be, but I love distance running. Running has given me the ability to do something I never thought I could do. It clears my mind, it keeps me in great shape and it makes me feel great. There are some days when I'm driving to school and it's all I can do to stay in the car because it's one of those gorgeous mornings and I want to be out running. I'm now forty-two years old. I have two children, boys ages twelve and fourteen, and two stepsons and a step-grandson.

Once school was out I began running by Melissa's grave. A student had placed a pinwheel on her burial place the day of the funeral. It seemed as though that pinwheel was always blowing, as though Melissa were waving at me.

Life is short and we have

never too much time

for gladdening the hearts

of those who are travelling

the dark journey with us.

Oh be swift to love,

make haste to be kind!

— Henri Frederick Amiel

Tommy Burns

This is how my friend Tommy died — alone, in a New Orleans hospital, far from his New York home, just hours after doctors had assured his fiancée and family that the blood clots that had traveled from his back to his heart and killed him were under control. He was forty-one.

This is how he lived . . .

Tommy Burns was, hands down, the funniest person I've ever met. He owned two restaurants in Manhattan, in the Hell's Kitchen area just west of Times Square. The Streetcar Café was a small bar and grill, a late-night hangout for actors, bartenders and neighborhood regulars who stopped by to drink, talk, be insulted and watch the Yankees on TV. The Delta Grill was a bigger operation, but just as casual. It was on 48th and Ninth, opened just before the Disney Corporation bought up most of Times Square and turned it into a giant theme park. Hell's Kitchen began to gentrify and the area swarmed with tourists, business people and couples out on dates. Business was so good that Tom and his partner had branched out, and were opening another Delta Grill in Baltimore. Hell's Kitchen became the place to be, and Tommy Burns was riding the wave.

Tommy was from a large Irish-Catholic family in New Jersey — he had seven brothers and sisters, and eleven nieces and nephews. He was the prototypical Jersey wise guy. He had a surprisingly quick wit and reveled in practical jokes — the dumber the better. Tommy was one of those guys who knew everybody in town and could always be counted on with a joke and a drink when life got a little harsh. Sometimes it seemed that Tommy, rooted in his own large family, decided to expand that family by taking in all the stray people he met in Manhattan, and then took the role of the pain-in-the-butt big brother.

Tommy loved his fiancée, Myra, his family, the New York Yankees and running marathons. I met Tommy five years ago when we were bartending at the same restaurant. He'd just opened Streetcar, and was working part-time at another restaurant to help support his new place. I'd just come back to New York after a year in Denver, and didn't know many people. Tommy found out that I used to be a runner and convinced me that we should do a marathon together.

"You and me, we're a lot alike," he said. "Yeah," I replied. "Except that you run marathons an hour faster than I do." (That, and the fact that he'd done over thirty of them — and I'd done two.)

Tom also loved to travel, so it became inevitable that he would combine his loves and invite his friends on trips where he could run marathons and everyone else could party. It was also inevitable that he would convince me that a marathon in a city far away wouldn't hurt half as much as a marathon in New York. He was wrong.

"You want to explain to my wife that I'm going away for five days of drinking beer and running?" I asked. "Bring her!" he said.

My wife demurred, but Tom and I were off to Chicago for my first marathon in twelve years. We met up with another group of Tom's friends, a running club from New Jersey, and spent most of the weekend searching for the coldest beer and the best music.

"You want to explain to my wife that I'm going away for five days of drinking beer and running?" I asked.

Tom insisted on buying me dinner the night before the race. There were giant pasta parties going on all over Chicago, but Tom insisted he knew a better way. He said he had a friend who worked at the best steakhouse in Chicago. "Aren't you supposed to eat pasta the night before a race?" I asked. Tom gave me a pitying look. "That's kind of '80s," he said. "The big thing now is protein. Especially before a race."

We went, and Tom ordered me the biggest steak on the menu. I didn't notice until later that evening, that Tom had only a tiny filet with his big baked potato, pasta and salad.

The next morning we lined up with all the other runners at the start, and Tom came over to offer me some last words of advice: "Don't go out too fast the first ten miles," he said. "Save it for the end." I nodded.

He started to jog away, and then came back: "Oh, and that giant steak you had last night? It's gonna come back up around mile eleven, so try to stay over to the side of the road."

He flashed me a huge grin and trotted off. The steak stayed down, but I was sure aware of it! I finished forty-five minutes behind Tom. I came home tired, sore and ecstatic.

And also ready to end my marathon career, until the next week, when Tom mentioned that the New Orleans Marathon was only four months away. This time Tom insisted that I bring my wife, since his then-girlfriend Myra was coming,

> "Oh, and that giant steak you had last night? It's gonna come back up around mile eleven, so try to stay over to the side of the road."

along with a huge group of his friends. Tom figured that we would combine the race with a little research and development on Bourbon Street for the soon-to-open Delta Grill.

So we all flew to New Orleans. I thought Tom and I were being remarkably well-behaved on the trip until my wife looked up from her breakfast one morning and remarked, "You guys really spend a lot of time in bars, don't you?"

But Tom charmed even my wife, who doesn't have a lot of use for around 99% of my friends.

One night, long after that trip, I came home just a teeny bit later than I had promised. My wife asked where I had been and I knew I was caught. "I was," I admitted, "out with Tom Burns." Her face lit up with a smile. "Oh," she said. "How's Tommy? I love him!" And just like that I was off the hook.

Four months after the New Orleans race we were on another plane, heading to Alaska for the Anchorage Marathon. That time it was just Tom Burns, Tom Sullivan (Tom's friend and business partner) and me. We were booked into a rundown motel on the outskirts of Anchorage, just across the highway from a strip club and next door to a minor league baseball field. We watched baseball every night, although I stayed away from the hot dogs and hamburgers before the race. On this trip I quickly learned the rules of traveling with Tom:

- Always check your carry-on luggage for phone books or any other heavy object Tom might have stuffed into it.

- Only drink bottled water or beer, so you could detect Tabasco sauce, salt, pepper or anything else he might try to dump into your drink when you weren't looking.

- Never answer the hotel's 4:00 AM wake-up call (the one he had conveniently ordered for you).

- Always shower with one eye on the door, so you would know when he was sneaking into the bathroom to dump a bucket of room service ice on you.

Of course there were ways to fight back. You could turn on the shower in your room and wait behind the bathroom door for the inevitable attack. Then, after he'd dumped cold water into the empty shower stall, you could nail him with your own bucket of ice water. Or, you could wait until Tom pulled up in front of the Delta Grill, got out of his taxi and, as he was walking in, turn all the TV sets in the restaurant from the Yankees game to the Mets.

The only thing Tom loved as much as torturing his friends was helping out the less fortunate. He used his marathons to get pledges from his friends and customers to raise money for leukemia research, arranged trips to Yankee Stadium for disadvantaged kids, and consistently donated money and food from the Delta Grill to whichever charity asked.

Which is probably why Tom's funeral mass filled up the midtown church where it was held. The seats were all filled an hour before the service and standing room was gone soon after. Tom Sullivan, Tommy's business partner, stood to give the eulogy. He looked out at the overflowing crowd of mourners. "Tommy," he said, "would kill me for not having a cover charge."

Tom had asked Myra to marry him on New Year's Eve. One week later, Tom, Myra and Tom Sullivan flew to New Orleans to pick up furnishings for the Baltimore Delta Grill. Tom complained of back pains and checked himself into a hospital on Wednesday. The doctors performed tests all week until they finally found a blood clot in his back. They told Tom on Sunday that he would be out of the hospital in a few more days. Tom was dead on Monday morning.

> He looked out at the overflowing crowd of mourners. "Tommy," he said, "would kill me for not having a cover charge."

After the service, my wife and I drove forty-five minutes north of the city. Tom's family priest read a prayer as Tom Burns, life long Yankees fan, was buried in the same cemetery as Babe Ruth and Billy Martin.

I woke up early the next morning and thought of something Tommy had told me when I was getting ready for my first marathon. "Sometimes," he said, "I feel like running's about the only thing that keeps me from going insane."

I left my wife sleeping in bed, laced up my shoes and walked outside. Then I pulled my Yankees cap low over my forehead and began a slow jog into the frigid January morning.

By Richard Barker
New York City, NY

Tommy Burns finishing the 1998 New York City Marathon.